My First Book about the Cat Alphabet

Amazing Animal Books
Children's Picture Books

By Molly Davidson

Mendon Cottage Books

JD-Biz Publishing

Read More Amazing Animal Books

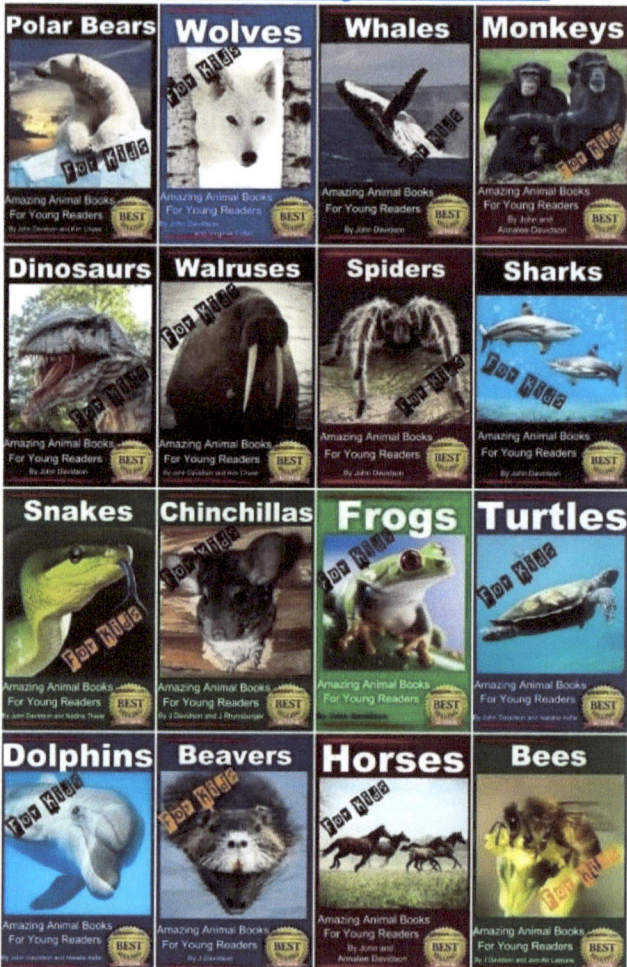

Purchase at Amazon.com

Download Free Books!
http://MendonCottageBooks.com

Some Cat Facts

To start out our book about cats, I have included a few interesting facts.

Cats are the number one pet in the World.

Cats grow and develop in one year, the same amount humans do in 15 years!

Cats can hear about 5 times better than humans.

Pet cats spend about 17 hours every day sleeping.

There are over 40 cat breeds, so look out for your favorite in this alphabet book. Also some letters do not have a cat breed, but others have more than one, I call them bonuses.

 is for an Abyssinian.

Abyssinian cats weigh about 6 - 10 pounds.

They are one of the few cat breeds that like to be high in the air, if kept as a pet; they need at least one very tall cat tree.

Its fur has the same pattern as a wild cougar.

A is also for an American Curl.

The American Curl cat gets its name from the way its ears curl backwards.

They are nicknamed "Peter Pan," because they like to fly around the house while playing.

 **is for a Birman.**

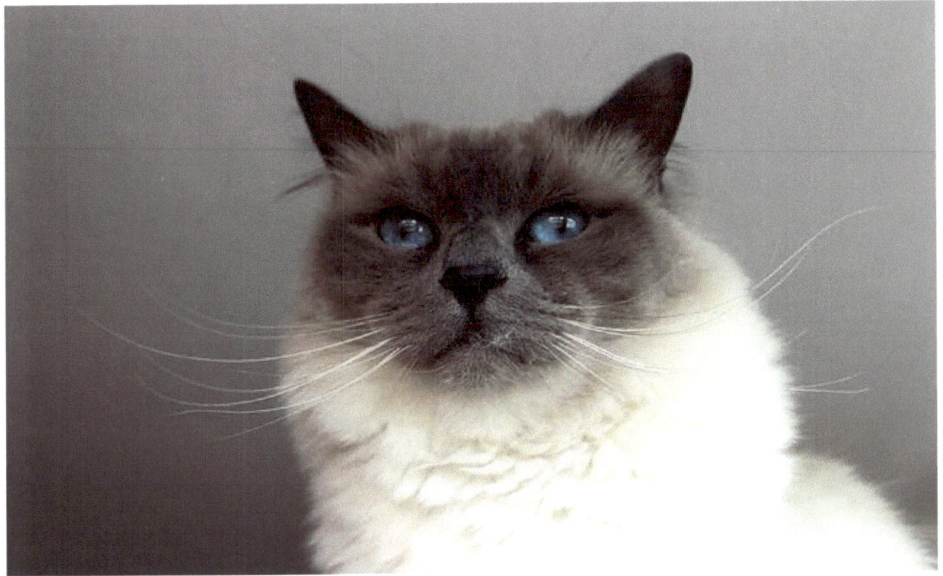

Birman cats are also called the Sacred Cats of Burma.

They talk very softly and love to be held and cuddled.

Birman's love to be with you and will follow you from room to room due to their curiosity.

C is for a Chartreux.

Chartreux cats rarely talk, they are very quiet, but can be silly when it is playtime.

They live between 11 - 15 years.

D is for a Devon Rex.

Devon Rex cats will always find the warmest place to sleep, usually under a blanket.

They love to play fetch, perform tricks, and like attention from children.

 **is for an Egyptian Mau.**

The Egyptian Mau, which means cat in Egyptian, is very playful and active.

They are the fastest house cats; running about 30 mph (48 kph).

E is also for an Exotic Cat.

The Exotic is just a Persian cat with shorthair and a different color fur.

They are sweet, calm, quiet, and kid friendly.

They weigh about 7 - 12 pounds.

F is for the Forest Cat, also known as the Norwegian Forest Cat.

Norwegian Forest's can weigh up to 22 pounds.

They are very gentle, friendly, and don't need constant attention.

 **is for a Himalayan Cat.**

A Himalayan is a mixed breed of a Siamese and a Persian cat.

They are very calm, sweet, quiet, and like to be adored by children.

I is for the last letter in a Somali cat.

The Somali is a sibling of the Abyssinian cat, so they also like to be climb and jump high.

They don't really get scared, not even by dogs.

J is for a Javanese.

Nickolas Titkov © <u>Wikimedia Commons</u>

Javanese are quite smart, quick, athletic, and playful.

They are the same as a Siamese cat, but they have long hair.

 **is for a Korat.**

In Thailand, Korats are known as good luck charms, and are given as gifts to new brides.

They do not like to be alone, so it is best to get two, or they will just follow you around.

L is for a LaPerm.

Bebopscrx © Wikimedia Commons

LaPerm's have loose, bouncy curls, which feel light and soft when you pet them.

They can be a funny cat, and they like to get into things, so be careful.

M is for a Maine Coon.

The Maine Coon started out as a mouser on farms and ships.

They are full size when they are between 3 - 5 years old, and some weigh up to 20 pounds.

Most Maine Coons live between 9 - 15 years.

M is also for a Manx.

Manx are a tailless cat, which was first breed on the Isle of Man, off the coast of Britain.

They are mousers, and also act like "watch cats," protecting your home from predators.

 **is for a Nebelung.**

© <u>Wikimedia Commons</u>

In German, nebelung means "creature of the mist," it got this name because of its silver, fuzzy fur.

O is for an Oriental.

Oriental cats are very loud, opinionated, active, smart, and playful.

Oriental cats are exactly the same as a Siamese, except they have different color fur.

They weigh about 5 - 10 pounds.

P is for a Persian.

The Persian breed has been around for hundreds of years.

These cats like to be treated like royalty; they like to sit in your lap, where it is warm, peaceful, and quiet.

 **is for a Ragdoll Cat.**

Ragdoll cats are super loving; they will just fall into the arms of anyone that will hold them, like a baby.

They are quite smart and can learn new tricks rather quickly.

S is for a Siamese Cat.

Siamese are described as looking like they're dressed for a masquerade ball, since they have a black face (like a mask), feet, and tail.

They like to talk loudly and express their opinion.

S is also for a Sphynx.

Sphynx are hairless cats that love attention.

Even though they do not have hair, they still need a weekly bath, and lotion on their skin.

T is for a Tonkinese.

The Tonkinese, called Tonk for short, is a combination of the Siamese and Burmese cats.

They are super friendly; all will follow you around until they get the attention they need.

 **is for a Turkish Van.**

Turkish Van cats don't really like to sit on your lap, but they will lay by you on the couch or in your bed.

They can swim and like to splash their paws in water puddles.

 **is an American Wirehair.**

Heikki Siltala © <u>Wikimedia Commons</u>

They have stiff, medium length hair, but it feels soft when you pet it.

X is the last letter in the cat breed **Selkirk Rex.**

Selkirk Rex cats have long, curly fur; they are also said to be a cat in sheep's clothing.

They are very active, cuddly, sweet, playful, and silly.

I hope you enjoyed reading the abc's of cats.

One last interesting fact, most cats do not have eyelashes!

Download Free Books!

http://MendonCottageBooks.com

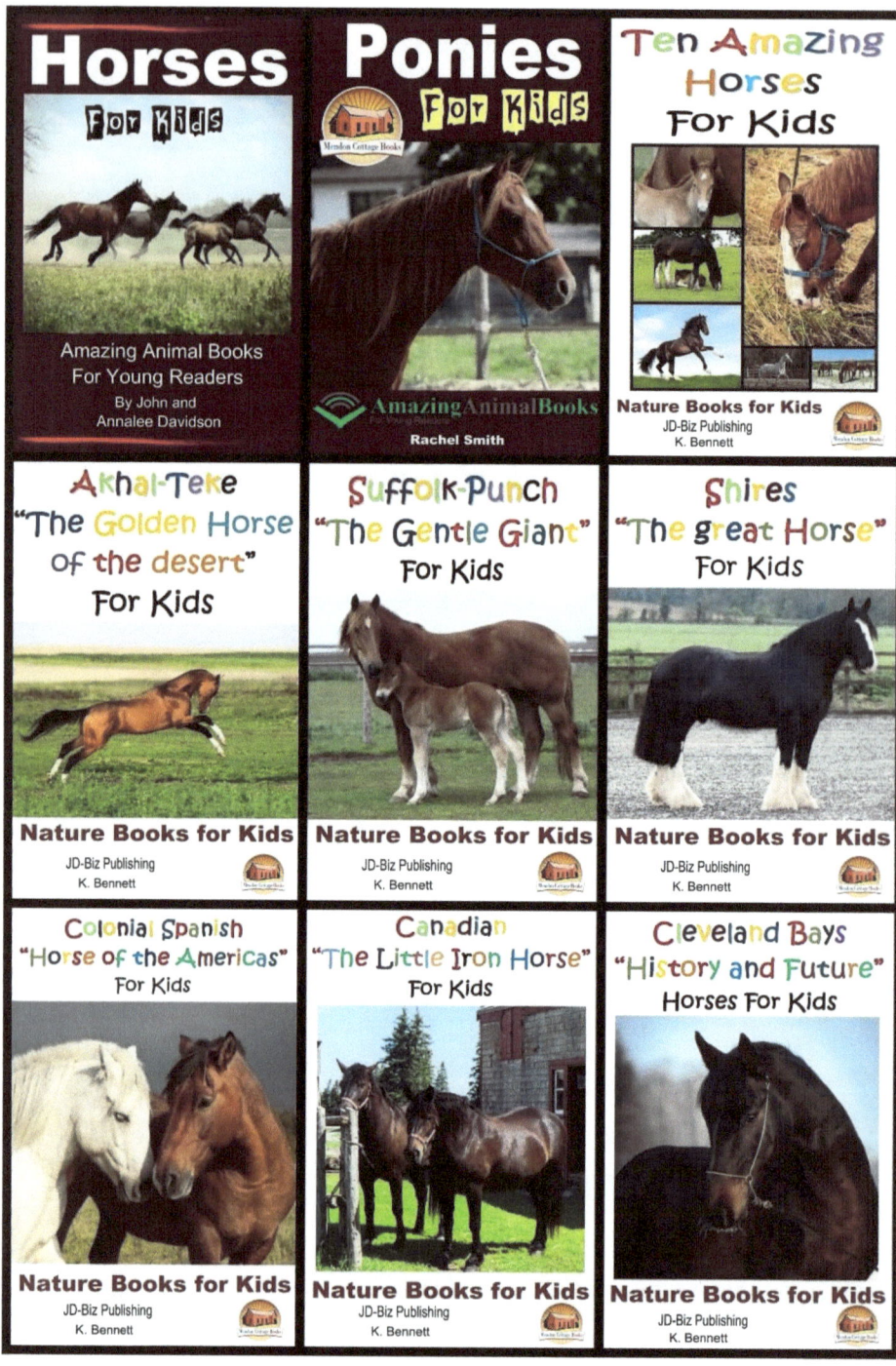

Our books are available at

1. Amazon.com

2. Barnes and Noble

3. Itunes

4. Kobo

5. Smashwords

6. Google Play Books

Download Free Books!
http://MendonCottageBooks.com

Publisher

JD-Biz Corp

P O Box 374

Mendon, Utah 84325

http://www.jd-biz.com/

www.ingramcontent.com/pod-product-compliance
Lightning Source LLC
Chambersburg PA
CBHW050903290526
45792CB00002B/682